The Heart of
His Word

A Devotional Journey
through Psalm 119

Carol B. Weaver

ordinary press
A division of
Sister Talk: Faith Ministries

Scripture quotations marked ESV are from The Holy Bible, English Standard Version®, copyright © 2016 by Crossway Bibles, a division of Good News Publishers. Used by permission. All rights reserved.

Scripture quotations taken from the Holy Bible, New International Version® NIV®. Copyright © 1973, 1978, 1984, 2011 by Biblica, Inc.™ Used by permission. All rights reserved worldwide.

Scripture quotations marked NLT are taken from the *Holy Bible* New Living Translation, copyright © 1996, 2004, 2007. Used by permission of Tyndale House Publishers, Inc., Carol Stream, Illinois 60188. All rights reserved.

Scripture taken from *THE MESSAGE* . Copyright © 1993, 1994, 1995, 1996, 2000, 2001, 2002. Used by permission of NavPress Publishing Group.

Be Exultant ©2009 by Warren W. Wiersbe. Used by permission of David C Cook. May not be further reproduced. All rights reserved.

ordinary press
carolbweaver.com
A division of Sister Talk: Faith Ministries
SisterTalkFaith.com

Printed by Color Corporate Printing, Inc. in the United States of America

Because of the dynamic nature of the Internet, any web addresses or links contained in this book may have changed since publication and may no longer be valid.

ISBN: 978-0-578-59978-6

Cover design and logo by Adam Simpson, St Louis MO

Edited and formatted by Samantha Luzader, Brooklyn NY

Author photo by Kayla Jan Photography, Tyler TX

To Jesus: The Word made flesh.
The One who captured my heart
and opened my eyes
to His Word made flesh
around me, in me, and through me.

Contents

Acknowledgments

First, to God our Father who patiently guides, cajoles, directs and corrects. His patience with me in embracing His call on my life is a blessing I don't deserve. I praise Him for His great steadfast unfailing love.

To those at the North Texas Christian Writers Conference (2008 and 2009) who gave their time, energy, and encouragement to writers pursuing God's call. The direction and guidance gleaned from these conferences started me blogging, improved editing skills, and laid the foundation for *The Heart of His Word*.

Thanks to my niece Samantha Luzader who helped me to edit and format *The Heart of His Word* as my first wholly self-published book. She helped me to make what was clear to me, clear to others as well.

Thankful for Stacy Boyer, my business and ministry partner. Our "iron sharpens iron" (Proverbs 27:14) relationship hones, defines, encourages, and solidifies my faith in God and His work in me.

And as always, grateful for my husband Craig who lovingly supports my pursuit of God even though he doesn't fully understand.

Introduction

Psalm 119, the longest psalm in the Bible, expounds the glory, wonder, and necessity of God's Word. In Hebrew, *torah* means law and it is found no less than twenty-five times in Psalm 119. But His law is not just a set of rules defining right and wrong. *Torah* also conveys the idea of manner or custom, as in one's usual way of doing something.[1] God's Word reveals His usual way of dealing with and relating to people. His *torah* tells us what's at the heart of His Word.

In the original Hebrew, Psalm 119 is written as an alphabetic acrostic, a literary device used in poetry or verse. Acrostics use sets of letters taken in order for the initial letters of the lines. [2] In the case of an alphabetic acrostic the alphabet is used. Psalm 119 has twenty-two eight-line stanzas to represent the twenty-two Hebraic letters: *Aleph* to *Taw*. Every line of each stanza begins with the designated letter. The alphabetic sequence of acrostics makes them useful teaching tools. An aid to help students remember the concepts of a specific subject.

In writing devotionals for Psalm 119, stanza by stanza, I embraced the acrostic style in which it was written. Each devotional focuses on a single Hebrew word as the central theme of the day's reflection and prayer. Here is where I apologize to those who know and understand Hebrew. To the scholars and linguists. I have no formal education when it comes to studying the Bible or its languages. In a way, God is my teacher, leading and guiding, making me hungry for certain information which leads to insights and revelation.

One of the things God stirred in me is a desire to know the original language. From a Key Word Study Bible, I became hooked on lexicons and dictionaries in both Hebrew and Greek. Today, most of my research into the words is through Logos, an electronic library for studying the Bible.[3] Using the Exegetical Guide, I looked for a focus for each devotional, making sure from

---

[1] James Swanson, *Dictionary of Biblical Languages with Semantic Domains : Hebrew (Old Testament)* (Oak Harbor: Logos Research Systems, Inc., 1997).
[2] Inc Merriam-Webster, *Merriam-Webster's Collegiate Dictionary.* (Springfield, MA: Merriam-Webster, Inc., 2003).
[3] Find out more about Logos at www.logos.com.

translation the word I chose started with the right letter and was found at the beginning of the Hebrew sentence.

The process was prayerful and not wholly scholastic in nature. So, I ask for grace and forgiveness from the academicians who might find my "translation" of Psalm 119 an affront. Translations are difficult. Many times, there is not one English word suitable to reflect the meaning of the original Hebrew. I pray no one will be distracted from the heart of God's Word, because of my handling of the language.

Most biblical scholars consider the author of Psalm 119 unknown. Some believe it to be a compilation of David's writings,[4] which seems unlikely to me because of the intentional acrostic style.

Warren Wiersbe in his commentary on Psalm 119, makes the case for Jeremiah the prophet as a possible author.

> I have often thought that the prophet Jeremiah might have been the author of Psalm 119 and that he wrote it to teach and encourage his young disciples (v. 9) after the destruction of the temple. Many of the statements in the psalm could be applied to Jeremiah. He spoke with kings, five of them in fact (Jer. 1:2), and bore reproach because he faithfully served the Lord (Jer. 15:15; 20:8). He was surrounded by critics and enemies who did not seek God's law (Jer. 11:19) but wanted to get rid of the prophet (Jer. 18:23). Jeremiah was definitely the prophet of "God's Word in the heart" (Jer. 31:31–34), and this is an emphasis in 119 (vv. 11, 32, 39, 80, 111).[5]
>
> —Warren W. Wiersbe, *Be Exultant*

I love the thought of Jeremiah writing this Psalm, because it was a verse from his book I asked God to make a reality in me.

---

[4] Matthew Henry, *Matthew Henry's Commentary on the Whole Bible: Complete and Unabridged in One Volume* (Peabody: Hendrickson, 1994), 913.
[5] Warren W. Wiersbe, *Be Exultant* (1st ed.; "Be" Commentary Series; Colorado Springs, CO: Cook Communications Ministries, 2004), 102.

When your words came and I ate them, they were my joy and my heart's
delight for I bear your name, O Lord, God Almighty.
Jeremiah 15:16 NIV84[6]

And it was these words He spoke back to me when He called me to write for
Him. In the pursuit of writing I began a blog, *Jeremiah's Menu*, named after the
one who wrote the words I long to be true in my life. Not sure how to begin,
I used Psalm 119 as the inspiration for the first posts. These posts form the
foundation of this book.

Many years later, discovering Wiersbe's thoughts on Jeremiah as the author
of Psalm 119 came as confirmation to the leading I felt to polish and compile
these early blog posts in devotional form. His theory encouraged me to
pursue publishing *The Heart of His Word: A Devotional Journey through Psalm 119*.

Whomever God authored Psalm 119 through, this devotional is my attempt
to find an "a is for apple," "b is for bear," etc. hidden in the Hebrew
alphabet. It is humbly offered with thanksgiving. Grateful for His Word and
its impact on my life, for His Son who saves, and His Spirit who teaches and
counsels. I pray what He taught me will be a light for your path too.

Your word is a lamp to my feet and a light to my path.
Psalm 119:105 ESV

Carol B. Weaver
An ordinary Christian following an Extraordinary God

---

[6] NIV84, the New International Version 1984 Edition is no longer available in print, but this
was the first Bible I studied and "ate." It is a translation dear to me and often the one I
prefer to others. *The Holy Bible: New International Version* (Grand Rapids, MI: Zondervan,
1984), Je 15:16.

Guidelines for the Journey

Begin with prayer. When reading God's Word begin by inviting God into the process and acknowledging your need for His help in understanding Scripture. His Spirit alone teaches us truth and reveals insights.

Open our eyes that we may see wonderful things in Your law.
Psalm 119:18

Read the designated passage for the day. Don't read the devotional without first reading the Scripture: His Words come first. Read from your own Bible. Read any version. If you feel so led, read from more than one. Remember the Bibles most of us read are translations, His Word came to the writers in Hebrew, Greek, and Aramaic. It is the Spirit who truly translates His truth to our hearts.*

I meditate on Your precepts and consider Your ways.
Psalm 119:15

Read the devotional. Each devotional is based on an eight-line stanza of Psalm 119. Twenty-two stanzas each representing a letter of the Hebrew alphabet. From each stanza a single focus is emphasized. But know this, it was written by a flawed Believer in pursuit of His truth. My offering is not the only thing to be learned from the passages. Like Him, His Word is infinite. Multifaceted. He is a personal God. You may see something different. When you do, ask Him what He wants you to know. Test everything according to and in light of His Holy Spirit.

Teach me, Lord, the way of Your decrees, that I may follow it to the end.
Psalm 119:33

Ponder and Pray. Each day's devotional ends with a series of questions to help you consider what you've read and how it might speak to you personally. An opportunity is given to reread the passage, to listen, for what God is speaking to you for your edification at this particular time in your life. Close your time of devotion by returning what you've read to Him in prayer.

I have sought Your face with all my heart; be gracious to me according to Your promise.
Psalm 119:58

Journal. This devotional is formatted as a journal. After each day's writing, pages are provided for your own entries. Record your prayers, your questions, your doubts, your revelations. Journaling what you hear and feel is one way to firmly impress your time in His Word on your heart and mind. Returning to your journal entries helps you see where He has answered your prayers and responded to your doubts.

I call with all my heart; answer me, Lord...
Psalm 119:145

* Several versions of the Bible are used in *The Heart of His Word*, each one noted as follows:
- NIV84: The New International Version, 1984 Edition. This version is no longer in print, but it is the Bible in which I first discovered Him, therefore it is my favorite. Some of its translations are used in this devotional for just that reason. They are my favorite.
- NIV: The New International Version, 2011 Edition.
- ESV: English Standard Version
- NLT: New Living Translation
- The Message: A paraphrase of the Bible by Eugene Peterson.
- KJV: King James Version

Day 1

Aleph
Psalm 119:1-8

Aleph (ah-lef), the first letter of the Hebrew alphabet, is for "happy." *Happy are those… who walk in the law of the Lord!*

"Blessed" is also a translation for the aleph-word found in this passage, but English doesn't have a single word to express the true sense of the Hebrew. According to the *Theological Wordbook of the Old Testament* it conveys the idea of "envious desire."[1] So, an alternate translation for the beginning of Psalm 119 might be:

> **To be envied with desire** *are those whose way is blameless, who walk in the law of the Lord!*
> **To be envied with desire** *are those who keep his testimonies, who seek him with their whole heart, who also do no wrong, but walk in his ways!*

Oh, to be like the ones who obey God's Word. *To be envied with desire.* People want what you have. Doesn't everyone want to be envied? Learning about God and living His Word is the way to a life others want for themselves.

God commands His people to keep His precepts, statutes, and rules with great care.

> *You have commanded your precepts to be kept diligently.*
> Psalm 119:4 ESV

But rest assured, He's not keeping score, taking names, or determining your worthiness to enter heaven. He commands us to be steadfast in following His rules because He wants us to be happy, blessed, joy-full. He cares about our welfare, our being, our life.

---

[1] Victor P. Hamilton, "183 אָשַׁר," ed. R. Laird Harris, Gleason L. Archer Jr., and Bruce K. Waltke, *Theological Wordbook of the Old Testament* (Chicago: Moody Press, 1999), 80.

We will never be worthy to enter His presence based on our own merit. We are only worth pursuing in His sight because He loves us. He can't stand idly by and watch us chase after what will destroy us.

He sent Jesus, the Word made flesh (John 1:14), to show the way, to reveal the heart of His Word, so we might be saved from pain, sorrow, death... all forms of dis-ease.

Walking His way, obeying His Word, is a happy pursuit because it is the right way. The way free from shame! In the walking, not just the reading, we discover a multitude of reasons to praise Him.

There is no way like God's Way. His way protects, guides, and satisfies.

Jesus is the Way, the Truth, and the Life (John 14:6). Seek Him, get to know Him, follow Him. In Him is found the secret to the life everyone wants to live.

> *"I came that they may have life and have it abundantly."* – Jesus
> John 10:10 ESV

At the heart of God's Word and Way we find happiness, joy, and a life overflowing with blessing.

Ponder and Pray:

Who or what do you envy? Why?

What makes you happy?

Does following God's Way appeal to you? Why or why not?

Read the passage again.

When considering the psalmist's heart and passion for God's Way, what draws your attention? What words or phrases stand out to you?

Close your time in prayer. Choose one of the psalmist's desires and make it your own. Pray for this attribute to become a part of your life.

Journal:

Psalm 119:1-8

Day 2

Bet
Psalm 119:9-16

Bet (pronounced like "bait") is the second letter of the Hebrew alphabet or *aleph-bet*.

Bet is for "how." *How can a young man keep his way pure?*

To be pure is to be free from anything which makes you less than you were intended to be. "Pure bliss" describes a state of happiness where nothing is detracting from your joy in the least. No guilt, no fear, no jealousy.

Why do we want to know how to keep our way pure? So we don't have to deal with the fallout of living a corrupt life: guilt, fear, or jealousy.

A pure way leads to a pure heart: undivided, untainted, uncomplicated.

How did life get so complicated? Sin. Sin is something we deal with from the day we are born.

> *Surely I was sinful at birth, sinful from the time my mother conceived me.*
> Psalm 51:5 NIV

I stand corrected, we are sinful from before we are born. We are sinful from conception.

The rebellion of Adam and Eve infected our DNA with sin. Therefore, life is complicated. We desire things that are bad for us. We want what they have. We know what is right and wrong, yet the wrong feels right and the right seems oppressive. The enemy's deception entices us to continue the rebellion established in the Garden by our great-to-the-nth grandparents.

How do we get clean? How do we rid ourselves of the effects of sin?? The guilt, the shame, the pain, the discontent?!

By living according to Your word.
Psalm 119:9 NIV

The Word of God leads us to a life of purity. A life free from guilt, shame, and discontent. All things which steal our joy.

We cannot achieve this in our own power no matter what. Only through Jesus – the Word made flesh (John 1:14) – can we keep our way pure.

Jesus offers us the gift of grace. To receive it is to be given a new heart, a clean heart, a pure life. No guilt, no shame, no discontent. This is the joy and wonder of God's Word: Jesus. This is the greatest treasure there is to find in all the world.

Therefore, there is now no condemnation for those who are in Christ Jesus,
because through Christ Jesus the law of the Spirit who gives life
has set you free from the law of sin and death.
Romans 8:1-2 NIV

Receive Jesus, hide Him in your heart, pursue Him through His Word, treasure up all He has to say.

At the heart of His Word, He shows us how to be pure. Free from the dis-ease of sin.

Ponder and Pray:
What images come to mind when you think of the word "pure"?

Is purity something you desire?

What sin most infects your life? causes you dis-ease?

Read the verses again.

Which of the psalmist's words resonate in your heart?

Close in prayer. Ask God to bless you with one of the desires the psalmist expresses regarding His Word. Make it your prayer, too.

Journal:

Day 3

Gimel
Psalm 119:17-24

Aleph, Bet, Gimel. We come to the third Hebrew letter.
Gimel is for "stranger" or "sojourner" – a temporary resident.

> *I am a stranger on earth; do not hide your commands from me.*
> Psalm 119:19 NIV

When we enter God's Kingdom by faith, the world is no longer our home – it is a war zone. We begin to reside in a different realm under a different Authority with a new eternal destiny. Life instead of death.

God's Word becomes immensely precious when we realize we are transients traveling through hostile territory. Once we surrender to Jesus, the One True Lord, we become His servants and discover His Way is the way of safety. Jesus opens our eyes to the truth of our reality. Things are not as they appear.

In the Fall (not the season but the act of sin committed by Adam and Eve in the Garden), people, whom God gave rule over the world (Genesis 1:28), traded their Heavenly Father for the "father of lies" (John 8:44). They listened to the devil rather than obeying God. Since then Satan has been the "prince of this world" (John 12:31). An arrangement God allows for a time, honoring the choice of those He created. Those who gave away their authority over the earth to another.

However, the current regime makes the world a dangerous place for those who follow Jesus. God's Word provides the direction, counsel, and solace we need as we travel.

Those who do not know God live their lives deceived by the enemy. They heap scorn and contempt on God's people in numerous ways and to varying degrees. The "rulers sit together and slander"[1] followers of Christ. But we must remember flesh and blood people are NOT the enemy.

> *For our struggle is not against flesh and blood, but against the rulers,*
> *against the authorities, against the powers of this dark world and*
> *against the spiritual forces of evil in the heavenly realms.*
> Ephesians 6:12 NIV

The battleground we walk through is not physical... it is spiritual. We fight an unseen enemy – one we can only discern through the power of the Holy Spirit. We do not fight the way the world does, our weapons are spiritual weapons filled with divine power (2Corinthians 10:4).

Journeying through this world entrenched in spiritual warfare, obedience to God's Word keeps us on the path of life (Psalm 119:17). Following His statutes cleanses our wounds and heals the battle scars (Psalm 119:22). God's Word is our counselor and a source of delight (Psalm 119:24), an encouragement to face the daily battle.

Arm yourself with Scripture.

> *...the sword of the Spirit... is the word of God.*
> Ephesians 6:17 NIV

Scripture in the hands of the Holy Spirit gives us what we need to safely traverse the dangerous terrain for as long as we are here. Until He leads us home.

The heart of God's Word reminds His followers we are to be strangers to the ways of the world and keep to His sure way for our time here on earth.

Ponder and Pray:
When have you been a stranger? What was it like?

---

[1] Psalm 119:23 NIV

Since following Jesus, have you felt like a stranger in your world? like you no longer belong?

When you find yourself in a new environment, whether a different country, culture, or setting, what do you most desire to help you acclimate? Why?

Read today's verses again. Consider the psalmist's requests when it comes to navigating the world as a temporary traveler.

Which one echoes your heart's desire?

Make his words your prayer today.

Journal:

The Heart of His Word

Psalm 119:17-24

The Heart of His Word

Day 4

Dalet
Psalm 119:25-32

Dalet is for "way," as in a road or path. The way you journey.

Gimel opened our eyes to the reality of our transient travel through hostile territory. *Dalet* reveals the truth of our worldly ways and then shows us a better one.

> *My soul clings to the dust; give me life according to your word!*
> *When I told of my ways, you answered me; teach me your statutes!*
> Psalm 119:25-26 ESV

The *dalet* word for way/road/path appears five times in these eight verses. It's important to know the way we're going because our path determines our destination. Even aimless wandering leads somewhere, as does walking in the dark. Neither of these are recommended ways of travel if you have a specific end in mind.

God's Word reveals the condition and destination of *our* way: a sinful path leading to death. Apart from God and His direction we inevitably find ourselves in bad places.

> *There is a way that seems right to a man, but its end is the way to death.*
> Proverbs 14:12 ESV

Through God's Word the psalmist recognizes the destructive nature of his path, and he is "laid low in the dust!"[1] The light of Scripture has the power to knock us off our feet. But God's Word will not leave us face down in the dirt without hope. His law shows us the way to life, redemption, and forgiveness.

---

[1] Psalm 119:25 NIV

My soul melts away for sorrow; strengthen me according to your word!
Psalm 119:28 ESV

God cannot be deceived – He is the source of Truth. We, on the other hand, are easily deceived, and often live lives based on lies. His Word guides us to truth.

Put false ways far from me and graciously teach me your law!
Psalm 119:29 ESV

God's Word reveals the way to freedom and release from sin and death!

I will run in the way of your commandments for you set my heart free.
Psalm 119:32 ESV (alternate translation)

You have a choice. God's way or your own way.
Reality or lies.
Light or dark.
Freedom or captivity.
Life or death.

The path of the righteous is like the morning sun,
shining ever brighter till the full light of day.
But the way of the wicked is like deep darkness;
they do not know what makes them stumble.
Proverbs 4:18-19 NIV

At the heart of God's Word is the way leading to life.

What way will you choose?

Ponder and Pray:
While driving or walking, have you ever wandered without much thought and suddenly realized you didn't know where you were? or how you got there? How did it make you feel?

What about in life? Have you ended up someplace you had no intention of ever going? How did you get there? What did you do when you discovered you were spiritually lost?

Read Psalm 119:25-32 again.

What do you most desire, along with the psalmist? Why?

Using the psalmist's words, bring your desire to God in prayer.

Journal:

The Heart of His Word

Psalm 119:25-32

Day 5

He
Psalm 119:33-40

From *Aleph* to *Dalet* we now come to *He*, the fifth Hebrew letter.
He (pronounced "hay") is for "behold" or "see."

Look here!

This Hebrew word, *hinneh*, is an interjection used for emphasis to call attention to something, like a detail or an idea.[1] Many translations omit this word. The New International Version often leaves it out, but the English Standard Version, a more literal rendering, includes it in the text.

In this case, the psalmist is calling for God's attention to himself:

> *Behold, I long for your precepts; in your righteousness give me life!*
> Psalm 119:40 ESV

Today, it might be translated: *Hey, look at me! Over here!*

The writer wants God to see his desire to know and understand His way or law. The entire stanza builds up to this call for attention: *teach me, give me, lead me, incline my heart, turn my eyes…* The psalmist longs for God's attention in his life so he might know Him better and possess the life God promises.

Is this an effective strategy to get noticed by God? Well… yes.

> *For the eyes of the Lord range throughout the earth*
> *to strengthen those whose hearts are fully committed to him.*
> 2Chronicles 16:9 NIV

---

[1] James Swanson, *Dictionary of Biblical Languages with Semantic Domains : Hebrew (Old Testament)* (Oak Harbor: Logos Research Systems, Inc., 1997).

God wants to strengthen those who ache to know His ways.

Show God your desire for His Word through prayer:
Ask God to teach you. He will.
Ask God to give you understanding. He will.
Ask God to turn your eyes from worthless things. He will.

Show God your desire for His Word through obedience:
Read the Bible, consider what it's saying to you.
Act on what you know, be faithful with whatever understanding you do have.
Recognize and reject the natural bent of your heart when it is in conflict with what you know of His Word.
Close your eyes to worthless things, be discerning in what you watch on TV, the movies you see, and the books or magazines you read.

Show God you long for His Word and His Way through your prayers and obedience. Give God something to look at in your life and see what kind of attention you get.

After all, Jesus said:

> *"Ask and it will be given to you; seek and you will find;*
> *knock and the door will be opened to you."*
> Matthew 7:7 NIV

Behold the heart of His Word and He will give you the attention you desire.

Ponder and Pray:
How do you go about getting the attention you desire from someone in your life?

Whose attention do you want most? Why?

Consider your life. What does God see? Are you living in a way you want Him to take notice? Or would you rather He look away?

Reread today's verses. Look at the writer's desires, take note of the attention he wants from God. Make a list of the ones you want from Him too.

Seek God's attention through prayer. Use your list as a basis for asking Him to strengthen your faith and equip you to live a life that glorifies Him.

Journal:

The Heart of His Word

Psalm 119:33-40

Day 6

Waw
Psalm 119:41-48

In Hebrew, *Waw* (*vahv*) is not just a letter, it is also the word for "hook." Like a fastener or attachment, a hook, peg, or pin.[1]

Hooks provide a place to hang onto for support. In Scripture they are found in the description of the construction of the tabernacle (Exodus 26:31-37), the pillars were fitted with hooks for attaching and securing the curtains.[1] The secured curtains created a boundary protecting unauthorized people from coming too near God's Holy of Holies.

We also gain a sense of security and protection from the things to which we attach ourselves. These attachments can be emotional or physical:

I'm *hooked* on _____. (Fill in the blank.)

The psalmist in the *Waw* section appears to be hooked on God's love through the promise of His Word.

Lord, give me your unfailing love, the salvation that you promised me.
Psalm 119:41 NLT

To have an emotional attachment implies devotion, loyalty, or faithfulness. Picture a preschooler's favorite blanket or stuffed animal looking completely wretched: ratty, stained, threadbare. As long as the child possesses their particular attachment, he or she is emboldened to stand in the face of fear.

Then I can answer those who taunt me, for I trust in your word.
Psalm 119:42 NLT

---

[1] James Swanson, *Dictionary of Biblical Languages with Semantic Domains : Hebrew (Old Testament)* (Oak Harbor: Logos Research Systems, Inc., 1997).

29

But if unhooked from their treasured source of security, the toddler falls to pieces, shattered by the loss, panic sets in.

> *Do not snatch your word of truth from me,*
> *for your regulations are my only hope.*
> Psalm 119:43 NLT

I know the exact moment I became attached to God and His Word. He hooked me when I recognized my mom trusted Him as she lay in the intensive care unit of a hospital about two weeks before she died. With her words: *I trust. I trust.* God snatched my heart, and it was no longer my own.

The tattered blanket or one-eyed teddy bear is a worldly sort of attachment providing a false sense of security. It has no real strength to protect. But God's Word? It is power-full! true! trustworthy!

> *I will walk in freedom, for I have devoted myself to your commandments.*
> *I will speak to kings about your laws, and I will not be ashamed.*
> Psalm 119:45-46 NLT

God's Word provides freedom and boldness. It provides true protection as you walk through the valley of the shadow of death.

A child's security blanket looks so awful because it's a source of strength. The teddy bear one-eyed because it has been squeezed so tight – loved so much. How does your Bible look? Is it pristine and clean? Or is it worn? dog-eared? looking a little ratty?

We don't forget to take along the things that have us hooked. We can't. They are essential to our lives.

The only secure hook to attach our lives to, hold fast with all our strength, is found at the heart of His Word.

Ponder and Pray:

What has you hooked? Why?

To what have you attached your hope? your future? your security?

Consider what would happen if you lost your attachment. What emotions rise?

Read the passage again. Put yourself in the psalmist's place. Imagine his words are yours.

Do they feel true to you? Or does it make for an uncomfortable fit?

Pray for a heart like the psalmist's, one solely attached to… hooked on… God's Word.

Journal:

Psalm 119:41-48

Day 7

Zayin
Psalm 119:49-56

Zayin is for "remember."

Why do we remember? We remember to keep something foremost in our thoughts, not let it slip away. To remind ourselves. We remember because we are afraid we will forget.

A string tied around the finger, a neon pink sticky note, or a memo written directly on the hand are ways we try to remember things we don't want to forget. Birthdays, homework, groceries, phone numbers, laundry at the cleaners, loved ones at the airport, kids at school. Timers remind us dinner is in the oven. Alarm clocks remind us to wake up. Calendars remind us what day it is. Day planners remind us where we need to be hour by hour.

We need to remember things because they are important.
Important people.
Important activities.

The Hebrew word translated as remember includes causing something or someone to be remembered or kept in remembrance.[1]

In this case, the psalmist tells God to remember...

> *Remember your word to your servant, for you have given me hope.*
> Psalm 119:49 NIV

We have seen the importance of God's Word to our Hebrew friend — it is his source of security (see *Waw*). It is his hope. The New King James Version translates "you have given me hope" as "You have **caused** me to hope" (emphasis added). Sometimes it seems easier to dive into a pit of despair than

---

[1] James Strong, *Enhanced Strong's Lexicon* (Woodside Bible Fellowship, 1995).

to endure the suffering of waiting for something better to come along. But God's Word *caused* him to hope – gave him reason to persevere rather than curl up in a hole and die!

He wants to make sure God does NOT forget the promises He made.

> *My comfort in my suffering is this: Your promise preserves my life.*
> Psalm 119:50 NIV

Traveling through this hostile territory where the brokenness of the world causes suffering on many different levels, God's promise gives life. Reviving our hearts and our hopes!

> *Remember God… don't forget… I'm counting on You to come through! You promised!*

The writer then tells God *he* remembers. The wicked neglect God's law and it makes him sick! But he finds comfort in God's Word on his pilgrimage to the promised land… *he* remembers…

In typical psalmist fashion, he set God's laws to music – they are his theme song.

> *Your statutes have been my songs in the house of my sojourning.*
> Psalm 119:54 ESV

The psalmist remembers God's name.

> *I remember your name in the night, O Lord, and keep your law.*
> Psalm 119:55 ESV

To remember the "name" of God does not mean to merely recall the word "G-o-d." Remembering the *name of God* is to meditate on His character.

When we think about the name of an object or a person we don't recall the letters and sounds of their name, what comes to mind is everything their name represents. It gives us a picture of something or someone we know.

For example, one may ask: *What do you think of spinach?*
A quick response is often: *I hate spinach!*

The person responding didn't think about the letters of the word "spinach." They clearly considered what spinach **is***:* slimy, green, yucky tasting stuff!

So, to remember God's *name* at night on your bed, is to contemplate who He *is* – His character. He is good, faithful, true to His Word, incapable of lying, almighty, loving, gracious, compassionate, ever-present… Because the psalmist remembers God's name he chooses to keep His law.

Keeping His law, following His way, is totally worth it. Any ridicule, any humiliation, any mocking because of obedience to our Savior is worth it.

> *This blessing has fallen to me, that I have kept your precepts.*
> Psalm 119:56 ESV

Remember God's name.
Obey His Word.
He remembers His servants.

> *See, I have engraved you on the palms of my hands; your walls are ever before me.*
> Isaiah 49:16 NIV

At the heart of God's Word is the reason to remember Him: The blessing of His remembering us.

Ponder and Pray:
Consider a time you forgot something important. How did you feel in the realization of forgetting? What were the consequences?

How do you remember important things? people?

Do you believe God ever forgets you? How does that make you feel?

Read Psalm 119:49-56 again. Listen for the psalmist's heart to be remembered by God. Hear the blessings of remembering Him and His promises.

Ask God to remember you, share any fears of being forgotten, thank Him for the blessing of His remembrance of you.

Remember who He is by closing your prayer in praise of His name.

Journal:

Psalm 119:49-56

The Heart of His Word

Day 8

Heth
Psalm 119:57-64

The eighth letter of the Hebrew alphabet: *Heth*. It rhymes with "mate," but begins with a guttural "h."

Heth is for "portion" – an individual's part or share in something, such as an inheritance or reward.[1]

When the Israelites entered the Promised Land, each family received a designated "portion" of ground. It belonged to them legally. Their allotted inheritance was their home, their livelihood – a precious symbol of freedom.

All the families received acreage except the Levites who were appointed as priests. They received God as their portion (see Deuteronomy 10:9 and Numbers 18:20). Perhaps the psalmist was a Levite or at least had the heart of one: *You are my portion, Lord....*[2]

The Levites were the only ones who could enter the temple – the dwelling place of God's presence among His people. This family of priests had a special relationship with God. They served Him by caring for the temple, and they served His people by interceding before God on their behalf. Land was not their inheritance, God was.

In Christ, we too are chosen to be part of a royal priesthood.

But you are a chosen people, a royal priesthood, a holy nation,
God's special possession, that you may declare the praises of him
who called you out of darkness into his wonderful light.
1Peter 2:9 NIV

---

[1] James Swanson, *Dictionary of Biblical Languages with Semantic Domains : Hebrew (Old Testament)* (Oak Harbor: Logos Research Systems, Inc., 1997).
[2] Psalm 119:57 NIV

Just like the Levites, the inheritance we gain is not material. There is no plot of land, nothing physical to claim as our own. Upon receiving Christ Jesus as Lord, we enter the Kingdom of God.

The Kingdom of God is not a place – it's not heaven – it's a reorientation of authority. God is spirit (John 4:24), therefore He has no physical kingdom, even though everything seen and unseen belongs to Him, His realm is spiritual.

The Greek word translated as "kingdom" in the New Testament is not to be confused with a place defined by boundary lines, it refers to royal power – the right or authority to rule over a kingdom.[3] Becoming a citizen of God's Kingdom moves us out from under the authority of the world and into His.

Our inheritance in the Kingdom is a proper, true, right relationship with our Heavenly Father. What we lost because of sin is restored through His Son. By way of the Holy Spirit we relate to the Father and begin to live by different rules. The rules of God's Kingdom.

You are my portion, Lord; I have promised to obey your words.
Psalm 119:57 NIV

We long for an intimate relationship with God – He is our portion, our reward, our inheritance!

I have sought your face with all my heart; be gracious to me according to your promise.
Psalm 119:58 NIV

Desiring to be on good terms with our King, we are quick to obey. In the midst of attack, we cling to His promises. All hours of the night we thank Him. His friends are our friends.

---

[3] James Strong, *Enhanced Strong's Lexicon* (Woodside Bible Fellowship, 1995).

Paul, an apostle and writer of many of the letters in the New Testament, put great confidence in his religious background and pedigree, until he came face-to-face with Jesus.

I once thought these things were valuable, but now I consider them worthless because of what Christ has done. Yes, everything else is worthless when compared with the infinite value of knowing Christ Jesus my Lord. For his sake I have discarded everything else, counting it all as garbage, so that I could gain Christ and become one with him.
Philippians 3:7-9 NLT

No longer do we need to cling to anything in this world. It has nothing for us. There is no greater treasure in this world than discovering God as our portion.

The earth is filled with your love, Lord; teach me your decrees.
Psalm 119:64 NIV

His love fills the earth... *Can you see it?*

When we consume God's Word, our eyes are open to His perspective, as we grow in our understanding of who He is and our relationship to Him. We begin to encounter *His Word made flesh* all around us. In those moments He lifts the veil between this world and His Kingdom – we come face-to-face with His love on a whole new level.

At the heart of His Word is the truth of who we are and who we are meant to be: His children, who belong in His Kingdom, with a divine inheritance which cannot be lost.

Embrace your eternal inheritance: *You are my portion, Lord.*

Ponder and Pray:
Have you ever been awarded a portion of something or received an inheritance? What did it mean to you? Why?

What does it mean to you to enter the Kingdom of God? Has it changed the way you live in the world? Why or why not?

Reread today's verses in Psalm 119.

Do you hear the psalmist's desire to embrace his inheritance as a Believer in the Kingdom of God? How?

Share your heart with God when it comes to fully living in His Kingdom now.

Journal:

The Heart of His Word

Psalm 119:57-64

Day 9

Teth
Psalm 119:65-72

Teth (pronounced *tate*) is for "good." Good being the direct moral opposite of *evil*.

> *Do good to your servant according to your word, Lord.*
> Psalm 119:65 NIV

God's Word promises good (not evil) to His servants. All that enters their lives is good.

Yet in this passage we also hear the word "afflicted."

It was good for me to be afflicted...[1]

Can affliction – severe distress, persistent suffering, anguish, torment – be **good**? It's good to be happy and admired, healthy and secure. But *afflicted?*

> *Before I was afflicted I went astray, but now I keep your word.*
> Psalm 119:67 ESV

Our Hebrew friend found good in the pain which brought him to his knees before God. He saw the error of his way and humbly returned: **now** *I obey Your Word.* And he sings:

> *You are good, and what You do is good...*[2]

Yes. I too join in this chorus of praise with the man who found affliction good. I've been on my face before God with the pain of conviction. Godly sorrow which turns a heart. There is no better place to be.

---

[1] Psalm 119:71 NIV
[2] Psalm 119:68 NIV

But what about affliction for doing good? being good? What do we do with the unexpected brutality of the world in the face of perfect goodness?

Jesus had no sin. He only did good, just like His Father. Yet He endured the suffering and pain of a criminal. And not just any old common criminal. The Romans restricted crucifixion for use on slaves, because it was considered too barbaric for citizens. Universally it was recognized as the most horrible and disgraceful form of execution.[3]

The single perfectly good, innocent Man underwent the most horrible death, unjustly convicted by the world and His church.

Yet, God, in His glorious power, used it to bring forth good news. Really good news. From what appeared a disastrous end for the Messiah, came a glorious resurrection, and a way of redemption for anyone who believes.

By sending his own Son in the likeness of sinful flesh and for sin, he condemned sin in the flesh, in order that the righteous requirement of the law might be fulfilled in us, who walk not according to the flesh but according to the Spirit.
Romans 8:3-4 ESV

The goodness of God remains powerful in a world we gave over to evil in the wake of our rebellion. God's power turns the painful consequences of sin, the perverse actions of man, and the brokenness of the world into tools for good in His hands. What the enemy intends for harm, God allows and intends for good to bring about His purpose – the saving of many lives (Genesis 50:20).

*And we know that in **all** things God works for the **good** of those who love him, who have been called according to his purpose.*
Romans 8:28 NIV (emphasis added)

---

[3] Walter A. Elwell and Philip Wesley Comfort, *Tyndale Bible Dictionary* (Tyndale reference library; Wheaton, IL: Tyndale House Publishers, 2001), 337.

The heart of His Word reveals an indestructible good which will not be overcome: He is good and what He does is good.

Ponder and Pray:
Do you believe God is good? all the time? Why or why not?

Do you believe He has the power to take what is bad and use it for good in the lives of those who love Him?

Just for a moment, accept His power to turn evil on its head. What in your life would you most want Him to turn upside-down? What evil might He use for good? Imagine what it would look like.

Read the *Teth* passage again.

Do you hear the good wrapped up in His Word and the psalmist's desire for it?

Ask God to open your heart to the goodness of His way. Pray for the blessing of faith, which receives everything as good.

Journal:

The Heart of His Word

Psalm 119:65-72

The Heart of His Word

Day 10

Yodh
Psalm 119:73-80

Yodh (rhymes with "mode") is for "hand."

Hands. They create and destroy. They caress and claw.
They can express victory and defeat; need and plenty.

They symbolize the source of blessing or cursing: *from his hand...*
Represent control: *it's in your hands...*
Or lack thereof: *it's out of my hands...*

They reveal innocence: *He has clean hands...*
And guilt: *He has blood on his hands...*

Hands. It all depends on who they belong to.

> *Your hands made me and formed me;*
> *give me understanding to learn your commands.*
> Psalm 119:73 NIV

The hands of God: Creator, Judge, King of kings, Lord of lords, the Almighty.

As Creator, His hands are busy. He forms each one of us in a fully hands-on approach – knitting or weaving us into being (Psalm 139:13). But His hands don't stop there. He has the hands of a potter, continuously shaping and molding our lives according to His will and purpose (Isaiah 64:8).

As Judge, His hand deals out justice and no one can argue with His judgments.

"See now that I myself am he! There is no god besides me. I put to death and I bring to life, I have wounded and I will heal, and no one can deliver out of my hand. I lift my hand

to heaven and solemnly swear: As surely as I live forever, when I sharpen my flashing sword and my hand grasps it in judgment, I will take vengeance on my adversaries and repay those who hate me."
Deuteronomy 32:39-41 NIV

He is King of kings and Lord of lords. There is no authority greater than His. None to stop Him when He stretches out His hand.

For the Lord Almighty has purposed, and who can thwart him?
His hand is stretched out, and who can turn it back?
Isaiah 14:27 NIV

Yet, His hands are also the hands of a loving Father (Matthew 6:26), a good Shepherd (Psalm 23). He reaches out to guide, nurture, and deliver from danger. In His loving mercy, He sent Jesus to rescue us (John 3:16-17). He has put all things into the hands of His Son.

The Father loves the Son and has given all things into his hand. Whoever believes in the Son has eternal life; whoever does not obey the Son shall not see life, but the wrath of God remains on him.
John 3:35-36 ESV

Apart from Jesus, it's a dreadful thing to fall into the hands of God (Hebrews 10:31). Only because of the Word made flesh, the promise of salvation through His blood and resurrection, do we have any hope. Any way to stand and face the hand of God.

The Holy One whose compassions never fail, whose faithfulness is great, whose love is unfailing. It is His law of love which drove Him to have His hands nailed to a cross.

"You have heard that it was said, 'You shall love your neighbor and hate your enemy.' But I say to you, Love your enemies and pray for those who persecute you, so that you may be

sons of your Father who is in heaven. For he makes his sun rise on the evil and on the good, and sends rain on the just and on the unjust."
Matthew 5:43-45 ESV

It is this law the psalmist longs to understand, just as we should. In our understanding we put our lives in His hands and become a witness for His love. His power. His greatness.

May those who fear you rejoice when they see me,
for I have put my hope in your word.
Psalm 119:74 NIV

Hands. The hands of God are trustworthy and good. Therefore, we can sing with the psalmist:

Let your steadfast love comfort me
according to your promise to your servant.
Psalm 119:76 ESV

At the heart of His Word we find the Creator who holds all things in His hands.

Ponder and Pray:
Consider your hands. Look at them. What have they done? What do they do? What do they reveal about you?

Do you have memories of the hands of another? What did they bring into your life?

What do God's hands represent to you? Why?

Read Psalm 119:73-80 once more.

What does the psalmist find in the hands of God? where does he place his trust?

Whose hands do you trust?

Approach God in prayer. Open your hands to His love. Pour out your heart into His hands. Ask Him to reveal the work of His hands in your life and for the faith to trust them at work.

Journal:

Psalm 119:73-80

The Heart of His Word

Day 11

Kaph
Psalm 119:81-88

Kaph, the eleventh letter of the Hebrew language, pronounced like the English word: *cough*.

Kaph is for *yearn*.

Yearn. Long for. Yet, it means so much more. Picture an adolescent crying out in desperate desire: *I gotta have it or I'll die!* Then you'll be close to the full meaning of the Hebrew.[1]

A longing which wears us out.

> *My soul faints with longing for your salvation...*

A hunger. A thirst. Without our heart's desire... we... perish...

> *...but I have put my hope in your word.*
> Psalm 119:81 NIV

God's Word promises deliverance from a broken world.
A brokenness driving us to Scripture for hope.

Hope is our anchor. Literally, the Hebrew translated as hope means "to wait, tarry."[2] Hope holds us in place, keeps us steady, prevents our drifting away, while we wait for His promises to come to pass in an ever unsteady and unpredictable world.

---

[1] James Swanson, *Dictionary of Biblical Languages with Semantic Domains : Hebrew (Old Testament)* (Oak Harbor: Logos Research Systems, Inc., 1997).
[2] James Strong, *Enhanced Strong's Lexicon* (Woodside Bible Fellowship, 1995).

My eyes fail, looking for your promise;
I say, "When will you comfort me?"
Psalm 119:82 NIV

The more time we spend in God's Word the more we see the world's darkness and depravity. Not only around us, but in us! Longing for His righteousness and salvation is driven deeper into our hearts.

We cling to His Word… dark corners are exposed…
We long for His return… we run to Scripture for hope…
A cycle drawing us nearer and nearer to our heavenly Father.

*Blessed are those who **hunger and thirst for righteousness**, for they will be filled.*
Matthew 5:6 NIV (emphasis added)

The Day of the Lord is coming when all things will be set right. Jesus will return in all His glory and bring the final judgment.

In your unfailing love preserve my life, that I may obey the statutes of your mouth.
Psalm 119:88 NIV

Our God is faithful. He cannot lie. He is true to His promises and has the power to back them up. It is His faithfulness which fuels our hope, intensifies our longing, and moves our hearts to yearn for His return.

So do not throw away your confidence; it will be richly rewarded. You need to persevere so that when you have done the will of God, you will receive what he has promised.
Hebrews 10:35-36 NIV

Wholly embracing God's Word and promises assures your ultimate satisfaction and fulfillment. The more you are in it, the more you desire it, the closer you come to God, the more you look forward to the Day of His return.

At the heart of His Word is the answer to the deepest yearning of your soul and the anchor of hope to hold onto until it comes.

Ponder and Pray:

Think back to one of your own adolescent angsts. Was what you desired really what you wanted? Explain.

Do you yearn for anything as strongly today? Why or why not?

On a scale of 1 to 10, 10 being a yearning you will die without, where does your desire for God and His Word fall?

Read today's verses of Psalm 119 again.

What speaks most to your heart? Does it echo the psalmist's desire? Or do his longings fall flat in your heart?

Go to God in prayer. Be honest about where you are when it comes to desiring Him. Ask Him to fill you with a yearning for His Word, His Way, His righteousness.

Journal:

Psalm 119:81-88

The Heart of His Word

Day 12

Lamedh
Psalm 119:89-96

Lamedh is for "to."

This small Hebrew all-purpose preposition begins almost every line of this eight-verse stanza. Bible scholars translate it primarily by blending it into the sentence. It's not literally seen, but the meaning is implied.

"To" seems the best translation when it comes to conveying the heart of the psalmist. A function word indicating the position of one thing to another.[1]

The position of God's Word to time: *Your eternal word, O Lord, stands firm in heaven* (Psalm 119:89 NLT).

God's position to people: *Your faithfulness continues through all generations...* (Psalm 119:90 NIV)

And for our Hebrew friend, his position to God's Word is the most important. At the heart of the stanza he declares:

> *If your law had not been my delight, I would have perished in my affliction.*
> *I will never forget your precepts, for by them you have preserved my life.*
> Psalm 119:92-93 NIV

Drawn to God's Word, the psalmist found his delight and salvation. In response, he positioned himself *in* Scripture. He examined it closely and saw no limit to its perfection:

> *Even perfection has its limits, but your commands have no limit.*
> Psalm 119:96 NLT

---

[1] Inc Merriam-Webster, *Merriam-Webster's Collegiate Dictionary*. (Springfield, MA: Merriam-Webster, Inc., 2003).

He saw God's infinite power and glory exemplified in the law He created. His sovereignty over everything seen at work in His ways.

Your laws endure to this day, for all things serve you.
Psalm 119:91 NIV

Because He is God, the proper position to take to His Word is submission. In His law we find life.

Our position to God's Word is one of the most important things to consider as followers of Jesus. He is the Word made flesh (John 1:14). The Bible is the only tangible thing God has given us as a means to know Him. It is the one thing we can see, touch, smell, and taste…

Oh, taste and see that the Lord is good! Blessed is the man who takes refuge in him!
Psalm 34:8 ESV

In the Word we "taste and see" the Lord – a taste test guaranteed to be good. The Bible is a generous gift from a generous God. One not to be neglected. An essential part of our daily spiritual diet.

At the heart of His Word, we find the blessings of coming under His authority as a response to seeing His love and faithfulness toward all He's created.

Ponder and Pray:
What is your position when it comes to God's Word? Is it something you see as essential to your daily life? Or does it seem irrelevant?

Do you position yourself under His authority? Or do you exercise your own set of rules when it comes to living?

Reread today's verses.

The psalmist sees boundless perfection when he positions himself in God's Word. Ask God to open your eyes and heart to the wonderful wisdom and way of His Word. Pray He will cause you to delight in His Word, which is the way of life.

Psalm 119:89-96

Journal:

The Heart of His Word

Psalm 119:89-96

Day 13

Mem
Psalm 119:97-104

Mem is for *from...* more or less.

In Hebrew this small word attached directly to a noun expresses the subject's relationship to it in some way. Choosing one word to best fit the meaning of the translations seems to be: *from*. (Most likely giving true linguists a twitch in the process.)

From, a function word, indicates: a starting point (*he came here* from *the city*), a separation (*the umbrella provided protection* from *the sun*), or the source (*this definition came* from *Merriam-Webster's Dictionary*).[1]

Our psalmist-friend credits his study and practice of God's Word for his distinction from a variety of people:

> *Your commands make me wiser than my enemies, for they are my constant guide.*
> Psalm 119:98 NLT

> *I have more insight than all my teachers, for I meditate on your statutes.*
> Psalm 119:99 NIV

> *I have more understanding than the elders, for I obey your precepts.*
> Psalm 119:100 NIV

God's Word distinguishes us from the pack. If we study it and practice it, take it to heart, we set ourselves apart from others.

Embracing and living out Scripture keeps us on the straight and narrow, separating us from unrighteousness.

---

[1] Inc Merriam-Webster, *Merriam-Webster's Collegiate Dictionary*. (Springfield, MA: Merriam-Webster, Inc., 2003).

I have kept my feet from every evil path so that I might obey your word.
Psalm 119:101 NIV

When the teaching comes from God, we know it's trustworthy.

I have not departed from your laws, for you yourself have taught me.
Psalm 119:102 NIV

Joy, pleasure, understanding, and discretion are all benefits gained from eating the Word and making it flesh in our lives.

Oh, how I love your law! I meditate on it all day long.

...

How sweet are your words to my taste, sweeter than honey to my mouth!
I gain understanding from your precepts; therefore I hate every wrong path.
Psalm 119:97, 103-104 NIV

Starting with His Word, we separate ourselves from the world, it is our source of light and wisdom in a dark and foolish world. All gained from His Word.

At the heart of His Word we find the source of what sets His people apart from all the rest: His Word in their hearts.

Ponder and Pray:
What sets you apart from others?

What do you gain from His Word?

How do you take His Word to heart? What do you learn from it?

Read the *Mem* passage again.

What distinction do you desire out of those the psalmist claims to have?

Make his claim of distinction your prayer. Ask God to fill you with a hunger for His Word, and to teach you to live it in a way which glorifies Him and sets you apart from all the rest.

Psalm 119:97-104

Journal:

Psalm 119:97-104

The Heart of His Word

Day 14

Nun
Psalm 119:105-112

The fourteenth stanza represents the fourteenth letter of the Hebrew alphabet: *Nun* (pronounced "noon").

Nun is for *lamp*. Or sometimes, more specifically *wick*, the part of an oil lamp which, when lit, gives light.[1]

> *Your word is a lamp to my feet and a light to my path.*
> Psalm 119:105 ESV

Light. A picture of knowledge, righteousness, and guidance.
Darkness. A metaphor for both ignorance and evil.
Creation was in the dark until God spoke light into the world (Genesis 1:1-3).

Light reigned until darkness entered Eden through Adam and Eve. They fell for the enemy's lies making the way for sin and death to enter all creation (Genesis 3). Since then darkness has ruled, except where those who know God bring His light into the world by faith.

In a dark world, light is an important commodity.
God's Word is the perfect source of light, when lit up by the enlightenment and insights provided by the Holy Spirit. It becomes a sure lamp to light our way.

Consider those in Scripture who followed God's Word – a specific call – into the darkness, the unknown:

---

[1] Leonard J. Coppes, "1333 נונ," ed. R. Laird Harris, Gleason L. Archer Jr., and Bruce K. Waltke, *Theological Wordbook of the Old Testament* (Chicago: Moody Press, 1999), 565–566.

- Noah spent years building an ark, no water in sight, for an unimaginable flood.
- Abraham left everything he knew to go he knew not where, all based on God's promise.
- Moses, forty years a shepherd, returned to Egypt to confront a pharaoh and set God's people free.
- Elijah, Isaiah, Jeremiah, and Ezekiel, all prophets following God in a dark world sharing messages no one wanted to hear.
- Mary the mother of Jesus said: "Let it be to me as You have said" – a call to a virgin birth that to all the world looked like an illegitimate pregnancy.
- The disciples following Jesus, not knowing it would end at the cross.
- Paul who learned what it meant to suffer for Christ.

Each knew the power of God's Word to overcome the darkness fighting to snuff out the light. Each could surely relate to the words of our Hebrew friend: *My heart is set on keeping Your decrees to the very end* (Psalm 119:112 NIV).

Think, just for a moment, about the difficulties of walking in the dark – no visible light.

> *I have suffered much, O Lord; restore my life…*
> Psalm 119:107 NLT

When we tire of suffering in the dark, we call out to Him for light. The light shows us a new way of life, but living as light in a dark world is tough – even deadly. Those who live in the dark find the light offensive, it hurts their eyes and wounds their pride.

> *…I constantly take my life in my hands…*
> Psalm 119:109 NIV

The enemy is always about the business of planting traps along our path.

The wicked have laid a snare for me, but I do not stray from your precepts.
Psalm 119:110 ESV

God's Word is the shining lamp lighting our path in the darkness. It helps us avoid the pitfalls set by the enemy.

We live in a world filled with trouble (John 16:33). No one is immune. Knowing trouble comes one way or another should embolden Believers to step out in faith. Our response to God's call and His Word should be the same as His Son who brought Light to the whole world: *Your will not mine...*

When it seems hard to walk in His Word, press on. It is the only Way to the light of life. Follow the footsteps of those who have gone before. Look to the Light. Let Him light your path. It is worth the effort.

Therefore, since we are surrounded by such a great cloud of witnesses, let us throw off everything that hinders and the sin that so easily entangles. And let us run with perseverance the race marked out for us...
Hebrews 12:1 NIV

At the heart of His Word is the lamplight which pierces the darkness, encourages faithfulness with the stories of those who've gone before us, and shows us the way of life.

Ponder and Pray:
Think about a time you were left in the dark, either physically or metaphorically. How did it feel? What happened when you tried to find your way in the dark?

What darkness presses in on your life today? What source of light do you use to push back the darkness?

Do you turn to the Bible as a lamp to light your path when you're trying to find your way? Why or why not?

Is God calling you to be light in a dark place? How?

Reread today's stanza.

Which verse speaks to your heart? Take it as your prayer. Ask God for the boldness and faith to step out against the dark. Trust His Word as the only sure light in a dark world.

Journal:

The Heart of His Word

Psalm 119:105-112

Day 15

Samekh
Psalm 119:113-120

Samekh, the fifteenth letter in the Hebrew acrostic of Psalm 119, is for "hiding place."

> *You are my hiding place and my shield; I hope in your word.*
> Psalm 119:114 ESV

We hide to seek refuge, to find a safe place during uncertain or dangerous times. We hide to find security and stability when the world wobbles on its axis.

God is found in His Word.
His Son the Word made flesh.
The Bible, a tangible place to run when everything else is unsure... untrustworthy...

We hear the psalmist pour out his heart to God: his hate for those who deceive, his reliance on Him as a refuge, his trust in His promises. God's Word is his only hope, so he tells the dissidents not to distract him from keeping God's way.

The world is full of the double-minded and deceitful. But in God's Word – in Him – we find unchanging Truth (Hebrews 13:8), a reality that anchors (Hebrews 6:17-20) and provides protection from destruction (Malachi 3:6) in the midst of the storm (Matthew 7:24-25).

At times it seems the wicked are winning, but He sees, He knows, His Word promises justice.

> *All the wicked of the earth you discard like dross, therefore I love your testimonies.*
> Psalm 119:119 ESV

There is nothing to fear but God Himself. Our flesh trembles before Him because it feels the pull of temptation. All of us are subject to the deceit of the double-minded. All could fall. Sometimes we need to run from ourselves. Hide from our own fleshly desires (James 1:13-14).

When we run to His Word, we learn what it means to fear the Lord and revere Him as the Holy One. The truth of who He is and who we are before Him turns our hearts away from the things of the flesh and compels us to pursue His Spirit. Seeking refuge in His Word, we discover the truth which exposes the lies of the world. Traps are revealed and by the sword of the Spirit we put to death sinful desires. In His Word, we find the perfect hiding place.

When your world quakes, spins out of control – either internally or externally – when you can't find anything to hang onto, run. **Run to Him!** Take refuge in His Word. Hide yourself there and let Him speak stillness into your life.

Then they cried to the Lord in their trouble, and he delivered them from their distress. He made the storm be still, and the waves of the sea were hushed. Then they were glad that the waters were quiet, and he brought them to their desired haven.
Psalm 107:28-30 ESV

Trust His Word. A sure foundation for our times (Isaiah 33:6).

As for God, his way is perfect: The Lord's word is flawless;
he shields all who take refuge in him.
Psalm 18:30 NIV

His Word. His promises. At their heart we find a secure hiding place to rest in a dangerous, dark, deceptive world.

Ponder and Pray:

What or who do you run to when you need to escape? What comfort do you find there?

Who or what do you find yourself running from? What makes you feel the need to find a safe place?

Sometimes we hide our hearts from others, including God, because we've been wounded by the world. Do you find yourself guarding your heart? hiding who you truly are? Why?

Have you found yourself untrustworthy? How? Do you sometimes need protection from your own destructive desires? your own double-mindedness? Explain.

Read the verses of *Samekh* again.

Consider how you feel about His Word and way. Do you love it? find security in it? Or do you tremble before it?

Ask God to move your heart toward His Word, to see it as a hiding place where you find security and safety: from yourself and the world.

Psalm 119:113-120

Journal:

Psalm 119:113-120

The Heart of His Word

Day 16

Ayin
Psalm 119:121-128

Ayin is for "servant."

> *I am your servant; give me discernment that I may understand your statutes.*
> Psalm 119:125 NIV

A good servant longs to understand the Master's Word so he might serve well.

A good servant worships the Master.

The Hebrew for servant translates both ways: servant and worshipper.[1] Equating service and worship is also seen in the New Testament.

> *I appeal to you therefore, brothers, by the mercies of God, to present your bodies as a living sacrifice, holy and acceptable to God, which is your spiritual worship. Do not be conformed to this world, but be transformed by the renewal of your mind, that by testing you may discern what is the will of God, what is good and acceptable and perfect.*
> Romans 12:1-2 ESV

Living a life perfectly aligned with and serving God's will is the way we worship Him. Service and worship cannot be separated when it comes to the heart of His servants.

The Master's Word is precious to the worshipful servant – he can't stand to see it abused.

> *It is time for you to act, Lord; your law is being broken.*
> Psalm 119:126 NIV

---

[1] James Swanson, *Dictionary of Biblical Languages with Semantic Domains : Hebrew (Old Testament)* (Oak Harbor: Logos Research Systems, Inc., 1997).

God's servants can't stand to see it broken because His law is love (Romans 13:10). All His law hangs on and comes down to love.

Deal with your servant according to your steadfast love, and teach me your statutes.
Psalm 119:124 ESV

To know His will, His way, His statutes, is to know His love. The Master reveals His love for the lost servant by buying Him back at the cost of His own life. When the servant sees and receives his Lord's love, worship must surely follow, and certainly does.

What may seem like an unlikely understanding from the world's perspective – a servant, a slave, worshipping the Master – makes perfect sense when one discovers the truth.

And in your steadfast love you will cut off my enemies, and you will destroy all the adversaries of my soul, for I am your servant.
Psalm 143:12 ESV

Serving Him, the One who loves and saves from destruction, fills a heart with humble praise.

His Word, given in love, captures our hearts as the salvation of our souls (John 3:16).

Servants… worshippers… enraged by the breaking of the Master's Law. Heartbroken… because His love is rejected.

At the heart of His Word is the truth of the Master's love for His servants – His beloved who He bought at the price of His life – and His servants' love for Him.

Ponder and Pray:
What emotions rise when you think of yourself as a servant? a slave?

What about the word "Master"? Does it evoke an attitude of worship from your heart? Why or why not?

Where are you when it comes to the Lord's Word? the Word of your Master? Do you desire discernment and understanding so you can walk in it? Or does it seem like an impediment to freedom? a restraint? Explain.

Do you see His love in His law? Can the two go together in your mind? Why or why not?

Read today's passage again.

Can you relate to the servant heart of the psalmist? How?

Ask God to fill you with a love for Him, His Word, His way. Ask Him to bless you with a servant's heart of worship.

Psalm 119:121-128

Journal:

The Heart of His Word

The Heart of His Word

Day 17

Pe
Psalm 119:129-136

Pe is for "mouth."

> *Mouth open and panting, I wanted your commands more than anything.*
> Psalm 119:131 The Message

According to *The Dictionary of Biblical Languages*, "mouth" is described as *the entrance orifice of the body for ingestion, breathing, and communication.*[1] It is the doorway for the fundamental elements of life: food and water, air, language.

The psalmist's panting reveals God's commands as an essential need for life. He so desires God's Word, he opens his mouth wide. Longing to be filled with His life-giving words, which nourish the soul (Deuteronomy 8:3), breathe life into the spirit (Genesis 2:7), and communicate guidance (John 14:6).

We are invited to cry out to the God who says:

> *I am the Lord your God, who brought you up out of Egypt.*
> **Open wide your mouth and I will fill it.**
> Psalm 81:10 NIV (emphasis added)

God is the One who fills. He encourages us to open our mouths wide and receive:
- Miracle words. Wonder-full words to live by and obey. (Psalm 119:129)
- Direction to steady our steps. Guidance away from the snares of sin. (Psalm 119:133)

---

[1] James Swanson, *Dictionary of Biblical Languages with Semantic Domains: Hebrew (Old Testament)* (Oak Harbor: Logos Research Systems, Inc., 1997).

- Teaching. Straight from the mouth of God, who smiles on those desiring to serve Him. (Psalm 119:135)

The *breaking open* or *unfolding* of God's Word enlightens those who long for understanding. The Hebrew for this unfolding also translates as *entrance* or *doorway*. Jesus is that opening, the gate, which breaks open God's Word and provides insight into the Father and His Kingdom (John 10:9, 14:6, Hebrews 10:19-20). He makes the way for even the simplest to understand.

Jesus came as the Word made flesh to communicate by example what it means to live a full human life (John 1:14). Through Him we see and learn what it means to love God and love others.

He is the Bread of Life (John 6:35). His body broken so we might eat and live. Not just for a day, but forever.

The source of Living Water is found in Christ (John 7:38). When we fill our lives with Him, we will never hunger or thirst.

Guidance and teaching, spiritual nourishment, and the breath of life come from Jesus. His Holy Spirit breathes life into our lives when we receive all He provides by faith (John 6:63).

Jesus, the mouth of God, the Word, the doorway to the essential aspects of life. The source of all we need.

At the heart of His Word we find the elemental requirements for life eternal. Open wide and receive.

'Man shall not live by bread alone, but by every word that comes from the mouth of God.
Matthew 4:4 ESV

Ponder and Pray:
With what are you filling your mouth, when it comes to nourishment? words? understanding? Is it life-giving? Explain.

What is the source of ideals and philosophies being breathed into your life? How does it affect your faith?

Consider your life. How would you describe it? abundant? full? satisfying? frustrating? empty? dark? Might the state of your life be related to what you are consuming? How?

Reread the psalmist's *Pe* words.

List the descriptions he gives of God's Word. Do any of these resonate with you? Do you want God's Word to fill you as much as he does?

Take the words of the psalmist and make them your prayer. Ask God to teach you to unfold His Word and find understanding to fill your soul. Ask Him for the blessing of satisfaction in following His way.

Journal:

The Heart of His Word

Day 18

Tsadhe
Psalm 119:137-144

The eighteenth letter of the twenty-two that make up the Hebrew language is *Tsadhe* (pronounced **tsah**-*dee*).

Tsadhe is for "righteous."

> *Righteous are you, O Lord, and right are your rules.*
> *You have appointed your testimonies in righteousness and in all faithfulness.*
> Psalm 119:137-138 ESV

God and His Word are never wrong.
He is always right.
His Word. Always. True.

Test it. The psalmist assures us His way has been proved and found trustworthy.

> *Your promises have been thoroughly tested, and your servant loves them.*
> Psalm 119:140 NIV

However, in a broken world bent on rebellion, it's hard to find righteousness. It's hard to find those who appreciate it. There are plenty who want to be **right**, but when they come face to face with His righteousness, they are appalled to find themselves labeled **wrong**.

> *"Your people say, 'The Lord isn't doing what's right,'*
> *but it is they who are not doing what's right. ...."*
> Ezekiel 33:17 NLT

The battle rages both internally and externally. In our flesh, His rules seem wrong (Romans 8:7), making it a fight to follow. He says we must crucify our fleshly sensibilities to do what is right. All around us, those who reject His rules, look down on, despise and ridicule, those who choose to follow them.

My zeal wears me out, for my enemies ignore your words.
Psalm 119:139 NIV

Our Hebrew friend finds himself worn out, consumed with passion to see God's righteous Word honored, embraced, obeyed. What he loves, the world dismisses, disregards, rejects. Surely his own human nature added to the tumult. As Jesus reminded His disciples: *The spirit is willing, but the flesh is weak* (Matthew 26:41).

It's hard to be righteous, to stand for right, when others ignore and our own flesh raises doubts.

We are left feeling weird. Outsiders. When everyone else fits in.

Trouble and distress have come upon me, but your commands give me delight.
Psalm 119:143 NIV

Loving what's right, in a wrong world, exhausts. However, I was reminded by a friend, I am not where I belong… and neither are you.

But our citizenship is in heaven, and from it we await a Savior, the Lord Jesus Christ…
Philippians 3:20 ESV

The struggle to wholly embrace our new citizenship under His righteous rule becomes easier with understanding. So, the psalmist cries:

Your testimonies are righteous forever; give me understanding that I may live.
Psalm 119:144 ESV

Live translated from the Hebrew also means "revive." Understanding His righteousness revives us from: sickness, discouragement, faintness, and death.[1]

Living righteously in a world gone wrong wears us down, weakens our resolve. But gaining understanding of His righteousness, rejecting what the world calls right, revives us for the battle. Strengthens us and blesses us with peace.

"I have told you these things, so that in me you may have peace. In this world you will have trouble. But take heart! I have overcome the world." – Jesus
John 16:33 NIV

He has already won the victory. All we are called to do is stand for what's right. Take heart. Trust in Him. Believe.

In a world of wrong, we find what is right at the heart of His Word, along with the power to revive us in our weariness. The strength to see us through enemy territory, until we make our way home.

Ponder and Pray:

In today's western culture, there is great debate over how to define what's right, what's true. Do you believe there is a right and wrong? What source determines the difference?

What most influences your understanding of righteousness? Explain.

Do you find yourself battle-weary from the pursuit of righteousness? in your own soul? in the world?

Read Psalm 119:137-144 again.

---

[1] James Strong, *Enhanced Strong's Lexicon* (Woodside Bible Fellowship, 1995).

Consider the psalmist's passion to uphold what's right in a world gone wrong. How does it compare with yours?

Like the psalmist, have you tested God's Word as a reliable source of what is right and true? Why or why not?

Ask God to reveal to you who He is and who you are before Him. Ask Him to bless you with the faith of the psalmist to embrace His Word as right and the zeal to live by it every moment of every day.

Psalm 119:137-144

Journal:

The Heart of His Word

The Heart of His Word

Day 19

Qoph
Psalm 119:145-152

Qoph is for "call."

> *I call with all my heart; answer me, Lord...*
> Psalm 119:145 NIV

...with all my heart... The psalmist calls to God. With every part of his being, he cries out.

We know from following his song, he has tested God's Word and trusts His Promise – he knows it's true. But here we see our Hebrew friend desperately calling on God: *Answer me!*

> *Those who devise wicked schemes are near, but they are far from your law.*
> Psalm 119:150 NIV

Our friend sounds lost. Bewildered. At his wit's end. The enemy closes in, successful in his advances, even though he is out of sync with God's ways.

Shouldn't obedience bring prosperity? security? That's what the world teaches. Yet God's way, the righteous Way, is met with hostility in a broken rebellious world. Obedience attracts persecution and injustice.

> *I rise before dawn and cry for help; I hope in your words.*
> Psalm 119:147 ESV

The psalmist anticipates the day knowing he needs God's help. With confidence, he puts his hope in what God says. In the original language the word translated as "dawn" can also mean "twilight," the transition from light to dark or dark to light.[1] So literally, the psalmist anticipates needing the

---

[1] James Strong, *Enhanced Strong's Lexicon* (Woodside Bible Fellowship, 1995).

Lord's help in both the coming day and the ensuing night, expecting persecution, antagonism 24/7.

For me, persecution (even in its mildest forms) causes confusion. Having believed God's Word, tested it for myself and found it true, I also cry out: *Answer me!* when I'm confronted. Called wrong when I've embraced what He calls right.

To believe I've grown in understanding His ways, gone forth with the light of His Word as He calls, only to be accused of being in the dark, brings bewilderment, dismay, doubt.

Have I deceived myself? Or has transformation occurred?

To the lost, have I become an aggravation? A new sort of stumbling block? like the Cornerstone?

> *"A stone of stumbling, and a rock of offense."*
> *They stumble because they disobey the word...*
> 1Peter 2:8 ESV

When I don't know if it's self-deception or transformation, I call... *cry out...* to God for Truth.

> *Hear my voice according to your steadfast love;*
> *O Lord, according to your justice give me life.*
> Psalm 119:149 ESV

Oh... So grateful He hears me based on His unfailing love and not my own merit, which is at best a disgrace. Boldly, I call out to Him according to His life-giving justice, a far cry from the judgment the world demands.

God in His great love, righteousness, and mercy established the law of the Spirit of life (Romans 8:1-2). In His economy, mercy triumphs over judgment (James 2:12-13) based on trust in the work of His Son on the cross.

He judges under the law of liberty. Jesus wholly fulfilled the righteous requirement of the law: death. In His mercy, He died for those who believe. And because He lives, we who believe live too (John 14:19).

He knows what's true. He reveals what's in a heart. By His Word, His loving justice revives a soul.

At the heart of His Word we find confidence to call out to God for help and understanding. In His Word, He provides the words to cry out for what we need.

For we do not know what to pray as we ought, but the Spirit himself intercedes for us with groanings too deep for words. And he who searches hearts knows what is the mind of the Spirit, because the Spirit intercedes for the saints according to the will of God.
Romans 8:26-27 ESV

Ponder and Pray:

Do you ever find yourself bewildered by the evil which seems to be advancing in the world? in your life? in the life of loved ones? Put it in words.

How do you respond when things don't go the way you think they should? What is your first reaction?

Who do you cry to for help? who do you call first?

Reread the *Qoph* passage.

As a follower of Jesus, do you expect trouble like the psalmist? or do you expect things to go smoothly?

If you are not yet following Him, does anything in this passage encourage you to pursue Him? Why or why not?

Wherever you stand with God today, ask Him to reveal His nearness to you. Ask Him to show you the spiritual reality behind the trouble in the world:

from global to personal. Call on Him from a place of humility. Confess you don't know, but you are willing to see and receive the truth.

Journal:

Psalm 119:145-152

The Heart of His Word

Day 20

Resh
Psalm 119:153-160

Approaching the end of Psalm 119, the heart of God's Word, we come to *Resh* (pronounced "raysh").

Resh is for "look" or "see."

> *Look upon my suffering and deliver me, for I have not forgotten your law.*
> Psalm 119:153 NIV

The cry of the psalmist:
> *Look at me God! Do You see me?*
> *Don't forget me. I have not forgotten You.*

In the psalmist's words we hear the cry of the faithful. Our Hebrew friend gives voice to those following God's Way in a broken world, where trouble is promised and the world provides the cross to carry all the way to death.

Even on this side of the Resurrection – death defeated, Satan disarmed, Jesus sitting in the place of Supremacy – the righteous suffer. The rocky road of refinement still a painful path in the resounding echo of the Good News proclaimed.

> *Now in putting everything in subjection to him, [God] left nothing outside his control.*
> **At present, we do not yet see everything in subjection to him.**
> *But we see him who for a little while was made lower than the angels, namely Jesus, crowned with glory and honor because of the suffering of death, so that by the grace of God he might taste death for everyone.*
> Hebrews 2:8-9 ESV (emphasis added)

His crucifixion and resurrection marked the beginning of a unique time in history. A time to live by faith, sure of what we cannot see against a backdrop of what we can see.

We cannot see the world subject to the Savior, but we see Him suffering unto death.
We cannot see His absolute authority over evil, but we can see evil hang Him on a cross.
We cannot see how He works all things for good, but in pursuit of Him we see our own suffering.

So we cry out with our Hebrew friend: *Look at me… deliver me… defend me…*

> **I look on the faithless with loathing,** *for they do not obey your word.*
> **See how I love your precepts;** *preserve my life, Lord, in accordance with your love.*
> Psalm 119:158-159 NIV (emphasis added)

In pain, we look with contempt on the lost who reject His Word. We cry out, reminding God of His promised Good News. We wonder if He sees what's going on. If He sees us. When everything appears out of sorts, and a far cry from being set right.

But His Word says: Live by faith, not by what we see (2Corinthians 5:6-7). He calls His followers to look at His Word with eyes of faith. Look at the lost with compassion.

> *The Lord is not slow in keeping his promise, as some understand slowness. Instead he is patient with you, not wanting anyone to perish, but everyone to come to repentance.*
> 2Peter 3:9 NIV

By faith, choose to see the Lord at work.
By faith, choose to identify with Him in suffering.
By faith, choose to continue to follow a Savior whose reign we cannot see.

Through our psalmist friend we experience and see God's patience. He can take our ranting, our complaining. We can come to Him with our heartache and pain. In fact, He invites us to pour out our hearts before Him (Luke 18:1, 7; 1Thessalonians 5:17).

In coming to Him, we take our eyes off self and place them on Him. Look.

> *Let us fix our eyes on Jesus, the author and perfecter of our faith...*
> *Consider him who endured such opposition from sinful men,*
> *so that you will not grow weary and lose heart.*
> Hebrews 12:2-3 NIV84 (emphasis added)

At the heart of Scripture, we learn how to look on His Word and see the world with eyes of faith. He shows us the only way to truly see.

Ponder and Pray:

What do you see when you look at the world?

What do you want God to see when He looks at you? Where in your life are you desperate for His help? Why?

What do you see when you look at Him? as the Father? as Jesus? as the Holy Spirit?

Does what you see of Him encourage your heart? or frustrate you? Explain.

Read today's passage again.

Listen to the heart of the psalmist. How do his words reflect where you are today?

Go before God with boldness. Tell Him about the way things look to you. Go with your complaints, your doubts, your anger, your fears. Pour out your heart before Him. Ask Him to open your eyes to see the truth of His Word and His promises. To see His compassion and mercy all tied up in His patience.

Journal:

The Heart of His Word

Psalm 119:153-160

Day 21

Shin
Psalm 119:161-168

Two letters left in the ode to God's Word. *Shin* (pronounced "sheen") the twenty-first letter of the *Aleph-Bet*.

Shin is for "peace." *Shalom.*

> *Great peace have those who love your law, and nothing can make them stumble.*
> Psalm 119:165 NIV

Peace. *Shalom.*

> The general meaning behind the root *š-l-m* is of completion and fulfillment – of entering into a state of wholeness and unity, a restored relationship.
> —Theological Wordbook of the Old Testament[1]

Shalom. Everything at peace – health, wealth, relationship – resulting in complete satisfaction, contentment.

> *Great peace have those who love Your law...*

Jesus. The Lamb of God. The fulfillment of the Law (Matthew 5:17). Loving Jesus provides great peace in every area of life. No matter what shape it's in according to the world's point of view, knowing Him as Savior, being at peace relationally with the Father through the Son, means trusting Him in His sovereignty and experiencing peace despite your circumstances. Not just a little peace. But abounding peace.

> *...nothing can make them stumble...*

---

[1] G. Lloyd Carr, "2401 שָׁלֵם," ed. R. Laird Harris, Gleason L. Archer Jr., and Bruce K. Waltke, *Theological Wordbook of the Old Testament* (Chicago: Moody Press, 1999), 930.

Jesus. The Word. Prince of Peace. Loving Him brings peace, *shalom*, to the soul, the spirit. Even when chaos seemingly reigns. When the rulers of this world attack without cause. No injustice, no evil, no insult can become a stumbling block causing sin.

The King James Version of this verse sheds a little different light on its meaning.

> *Great peace have they which love thy law: And nothing shall offend them.*
> Psalm 119:165 KJV

Those who love His law shall not be offended, our love for others will not be upended. When we love His law, the trap of self-righteous anger will not move us to sin no matter the offense. Understanding His fulfillment of the law through His Son keeps us in a place of peace with others and ourselves. He paid a great price for the world's sins as well as ours. Peace reigns when we recognize His sovereignty and purpose in bringing others to Himself through us.

In the midst of persecution, when falsehood rules, love for God's Word, praise for His law, restores peace.

> *Seven times a day I praise you for your righteous rules.*
> Psalm 119:164 ESV

His promise, the treasure of great joy (Matthew 13:44-46), is His peace.

> *I rejoice at your word like one who finds great spoil.*
> Psalm 119:162 ESV

The waiting only made possible through obedience (John 15:10) and its peace (John 20:21).

I wait for your salvation, Lord, and I follow your commands.
Psalm 119:166 NIV

To love the Word, to embrace the beauty of God's law, to praise His righteousness, is to know **peace**. *Shalom.*

I obey your statutes, for I love them greatly.
Psalm 119:167 NIV

Stop stumbling. Find great peace. Love the law, the Word made flesh.

Rejoice in the Lord always. I will say it again: Rejoice! Let your gentleness be evident to all. The Lord is near. Do not be anxious about anything, but in every situation, by prayer and petition, with thanksgiving, present your requests to God. And the peace of God, which transcends all understanding, will guard your hearts and your minds in Christ Jesus.
Philippians 4:4-7 NIV

At the heart of His Word… *Ahh…* we find perfect peace.

Ponder and Pray:

On a scale of 1-10, 1 being none, how much peace do you experience in your daily life?

What disturbs your peace most? Why?

How do you seek to restore or establish peace in your world? Is it effective?

Do you understand the psalmist's perspective of finding peace in God's Word? Explain.

Re-read the *Shin* verses.

Where can you identify with the psalmist? Which of his words voice your desire?

Take his words and write a prayer seeking God's peace in your life. Ask Him to increase your love for His law, His Way, His Word. Ask Him to lead you in the way of peace, no matter your circumstance.

Journal:

The Heart of His Word

Psalm 119:161-168

The Heart of His Word

Day 22

Taw
Psalm 119:169-176

We've come to the end of Psalm 119, the heart of His Word. Twenty-two letters. Twenty-two stanzas. The final letter *Taw* (pronounced "tov").

Taw is for "mark."

Literally, the meaning of the name of the twenty-second Hebrew letter is "mark."[1]

The word "mark" conjures up many images.
> A distinguishing feature or sign: good or evil, fortuitous or ominous.
> A target: *Don't miss the mark!*
> A grade: *She made a bad mark on the test.*
> An impression: *That'll leave a mark.*
> A signature: someone's *mark,* an "x," when they can't read or write.

As we come to the final eight verses of the longest psalm in Scripture, our psalmist friend signs off, leaving his mark with a prayer asking God to let His Word leave a mark on his life.

He asks to be marked with understanding...

> *Let my cry come before you, O Lord; give me understanding according to your word!*
> Psalm 119:169 ESV

He asks for his speech to be marked with praise, because God Himself teaches him...

---

[1] Ronald F. Youngblood, "2496 תָּוָה," ed. R. Laird Harris, Gleason L. Archer Jr., and Bruce K. Waltke, *Theological Wordbook of the Old Testament* (Chicago: Moody Press, 1999), 966.

My lips will pour forth praise, for you teach me your statutes.
My tongue will sing of your word, for all your commandments are right.
Psalm 119:171-172 ESV

Finally, he asks for his life to be marked with God's help…

Let your hand be ready to help me, for I have chosen your precepts.
Psalm 119:173 ESV

Our Hebrew friend delights in God's Word. In it he finds the path of salvation and deliverance.

Knowing His Word is the only way we know we are lost. The only way we recognize the Shepherd when He comes to seek us.

I have gone astray like a lost sheep; seek your servant, for I do not forget your commandments.
Psalm 119:176 ESV

May our journey through God's Word leave a mark on us.
May we desire the impression of His Word on our lives.

We may never write an ode to exalt His Word, but I hope we will take it to heart. Marked by His Word, branded so to speak, for His glory!

And you also were included in Christ **when you heard the word of truth,** *the gospel of your salvation. Having believed,* **you were marked** *in him with a seal, the promised Holy Spirit, who is a deposit guaranteeing our inheritance until the redemption of those who are God's possession –* **to the praise of his glory.**
Ephesians 1:13-14 NIV84 (emphasis added)

At the heart of His Word we find the markings of those who know Him, as well as those who reject Him. The way we deal with and respond to His Word reveals His mark (or lack of it) on us.

Ponder and Pray:

What most marks your life? How does it reveal its mark?

How has God's Word marked your life?

Do you know His Word well enough to hear Him as your Shepherd? What about when you wander like a lost sheep?

Reread the psalmist's words beginning with *Taw*.

Consider how God's Word marked the psalmist's life. List specifics. Write a prayer asking God to use His Word to make an everlasting mark on you.

Psalm 119:169-176

Journal:

The Heart of His Word

Psalm 119:169-176

The Heart of His Word

Afterword

May everyone who reads the words of *The Heart of His Word: A Devotional Journey through Psalm 119* be moved to go deeper into Scripture. All of Scripture, the words He's spoken to us in love.

From Genesis to Revelation, all is given to us so we can come to know Him and ourselves more fully. So we can grow in relationship with Him.

Jesus came as the Word Made Flesh to show us how to live out His Word by the power of His Spirit. By His grace He's made the way for us to receive His Spirit. Through Him we have the power and potential to become the Word made flesh too. Bringing glory to God for the building of His Kingdom.

I pray you are now left hungry for more of Him.
I pray you have a better understanding of what you will find in His Word and begin digging into it yourself.

I pray you will connect with other Believers in a faith community to consider His Word, to share revelations and insights, for where two or three gather in His name, there He is with them (Matthew 18:20).

My heart is for you to know the heart of His Word for yourself. The Word He's so graciously preserved for us and given us, along with the Holy Spirit who reveals its meaning and blesses us with understanding.

May it be so! Amen & Amen.

Ponder and Pray:
How has this devotional based on Psalm 119 affected the way you view His Word?

How will you continue to seek the heart of His Word? make it flesh in your life?

Ask Him to bless you with a deep desire to know Him through His Word by the power of the Holy Spirit, and to lead you to the resources and faith community you need to continue your journey into the heart of His Word.

Journal:

The Heart of His Word

Afterword

The Heart of His Word

About the Author

Carol B. Weaver lives an ordinary life in pursuit of an Extraordinary God. Following Him has led to teaching His Word in various settings and to a wide range of ages, leading prayer groups, and writing for Him. Carol has been published in The Upper Room and completed one previous devotional book, *The Heart of Bethlehem: A Twenty-five Day Journey of Faith for the Christmas Season.* She blogs regularly at JeremiahsMenu.com, where the foundational writing for *The Heart of His Word: A Devotional Journey Through Psalm 119* began.

Carol lives in the piney woods of East Texas with her husband. Four days a week she can be found downtown in a small shop she co-owns with a friend. The shop is the home of Sister Talk: Faith, a Bible teaching ministry she and her business partner formed in 2016. Their studies can be found at SisterTalkFaith.com.

Keep up with Carol at carolbweaver.com where she is learning to shine for Him and His glory.